Abortion and Healing

A Cry to be Whole

Michael T. Mannion

Sheed & Ward

All profits from this book will be donated
to organizations that have
dedicated themselves
to the healing of
women who have had
abortions.

Contributions can be sent to: National
Youth Pro Life Coalition Educational
Foundation — Healing Outreach.
Jackson Ave., Hastings-on-the-Hudson,
N.Y. 10706. (914) 478-0103.

Sheed and Ward™ is a service of National Catholic
Reporter Publishing, Inc.

Library of Congress Catalog Card Number: 86-60382

ISBN: 0-934134-35-9

Published by:

Sheed and Ward
115 E. Armour Blvd. P.O. Box 281
Kansas City, MO 64141-0281

To order, call: (800) 821-7926

CONTENTS

Acknowledgements

I wish to give thanks to the many who helped bring this book from dream to reality:

Discovery, Retreat Program Staffs — for their support, love and understanding.

Fr. Edward M. Bryce, director, office of pro-life activities, department of education, U.S. Catholic Conference, Washington, D.C. — for his strong encouragement.

Kara Eustace, Joan McLaughlin, Dolly Petti and Brenda L. Tine' — for forming a team of dedicated typists.

Wanda Franz, Ph.D., W. Virginia Univ., Vice President, National Right to Life Committee — for the extremely helpful feedback and rewrite assistance.

Dr. Jean Garton, President, Lutherans for Life — for her feedback, affirmation and many years of friendship and support.

Mary Anne Hughes, President, National Youth Pro-Life Coalition — for the many helpful suggestions and contacts.

Robert Heyer, Editor-in-Chief, Sheed and Ward — for believing in the need for this book and supporting it.

Fr. Thomas Legere, S.T.L.,M.A. — Retreat, Spiritual Director and author — for his valuable spiritual insights.

Mother Teresa, M.C. — for her deep insights and words of encouragement.

Ernest L. Ohlhoff, Exec. Dir., National Committee for a Human Life Amendment — for spurring me on to write this book.

Vicky Thorn, Coordinator, Project Rachel, Milwaukee, Wis. — for her important input.

Newman Center students at Glassboro State College — for loving me and being patient with me.

This book is dedicated

to the hundreds of women who
trusted me with their
stories and cries for
healing.

to my mother and father, who
taught me the sacredness
of my life and others.

Introduction

"I'm in bed trying to go to sleep and I'm thinking. I never thought my life would be the way it is today. I went out with a very cute guy who told me he loved me, although I knew we didn't have a perfect relationship. It wasn't right to have sex with him but I did. He was the only person who knew that I was pregnant and he said, 'you have to have an abortion — it's okay. We have to finish school.'

"The minute I left the clinic *I hated myself* and I wished that someone could have stopped me. Afterwards I felt like an empty soul. All of my life I was told what to do. Then comes the biggest decision of my life and I had to make it alone.

"Every day I think about it. I thought my mom knew everything. Sometimes when I'm out I wish I could go home and hug my baby and show it how much I love it. Well, we know I can't do that so what do I do? I have faith in God and pray for this sadness to end.

". . . it is very hard to express my feelings and thoughts."

This tragic testimony is from a young woman who had an abortion two years previous to its writing. Her words strongly indicate that to know something in our head is much different than to know it in our heart. One may know intellectually that abortion is wrong, but the emotional fears and terrors may outweigh that knowledge and prevent the heart from understanding and acting on that truth. In addition, the woman with these feelings may also have to face a Christian community with strong pro-life values.

Indeed, we of the Christian Community often find ourselves criticized because of the heavy emphasis we place on the value of the unborn human life. A defense of the right to life for the unborn child, however, also demands a support system for the woman who carries that child. The woman has many needs, as the above testimony indicates. Within a church group, parish, or with individuals, we cannot only moralize to the woman about what she *should* do. We must also offer the support, love, and compassion necessary to help her do it. As a church community we carry a

8

strong moral responsibility to assist her in discovering positive alternatives to abortion, and then stand by her emotionally and spiritually as she faces the reactions, opinions, and very possibly, judgments of her parents, friends, and relatives.

Our teaching reflects the fact that we have chosen to ratify in our belief system what our Father, as Creator, has done. If we really believe all human life is a gift from our Father, then it is sacred. If not, then we can dispose of it as we wish. It is important, too, that we understand that much of the criticism levelled against the Catholic Christian community for our strong position on unborn children finds validity in the eyes of others because they see us as deeply remiss in proclaiming the sacredness of life in so many other areas. It is certainly true that we must develop more of a total vision for the issues of human life. Be that as it may, I strongly feel our cries for the protection of the unborn are valid and that all life issues are intricately related.

More specifically, in the following pages, I would like to discuss some of the emotional, psychological and spiritual dynamics that I see operative in the young girl or woman who has had or is contemplating an abortion. My experiences in youth and young adult ministry in the Diocese of Camden, N.J. over the past 14 years have brought me in contact with hundreds of girls and women who were struggling to confront the confusion and difficulty of an unwanted pregnancy. I offer no trite solutions or pietistic platitudes. By these words, I simply hope to reaffirm my faith in a loving Father who holds us all in the palm of His hand. I dedicate these words to those girls and women, many of whom in their brokenness, taught me much about that loving Father. Obviously, I cannot condone the action of abortion, for I, too, believe deeply in the sacredness of human life. Through these words, I wish to rededicate myself to the ministry of healing which these girls and women seek so intensely and deserve fully from the rich heritage of our church, sacramentally, pastorally, and scripturally. We care deeply about the woman and it is not enough to tell her that what she's done is wrong. We must show her a way back. We must respond to her cry to be whole. This book is an effort to do that.

Without a doubt, abortion touches all phases of human life and its effects are felt in every age group, inside and outside of the family unit. Other members of a family system are often deeply affected when an unborn child is not permitted entry into it. If nothing else, the other children wonder about the criteria of acceptance and by what standard one is "worthy" to be born. Recent studies give evidence of increased violence and even infanticide in families where abortion has occured. Violence in the womb cannot be contained to the womb. The pattern often spreads to life beyond the womb. Dr. Vincent Rue is a clinical psychologist from California who has extensive experience in post abortion counselling. He notes the case of a young child who broke his arm and was having deep psychological problems. He knew that his parents had aborted his baby sister a few months before birth because she was "defective." It was logical that now they could do away with him. Adults wonder, too, though they seem to speak of it less, perhaps fearing that their confusion and uncertainty will make them less in their children's eyes.

Parents, sometimes unconsciously and

unwittingly, condition their children to justify future pro-abortion decisions in a profound manner. Children, at the teenage stage, may construct an extremely negative image of their parents which may not be accurate. This negative image is the perceived image that the child will act upon. "I just couldn't tell my dad I'm pregnant — he could never handle it! Besides, he told me if I ever came home pregnant, he'd kill me!" Though it may be idle rhetoric on the parent's part, or even reality in some cases, it may spring from a father's well-intentioned, though severely misguided efforts to discourage moral misbehavior in his daughter by pronouncements of severe threat of punishment. Perhaps such a tactic works in some families. I personally have not seen it lead to anything but further problems. Since the child's value system has always included the golden rule of discipline, "Never hurt mom or dad," the child may feel morally justified in having an abortion to "protect mom or dad from pain and hurt."

What is desperately needed in family life is a common mechanism for parent and child together to explore each other's feelings, values, real (not just perceived) levels of tolerance, compassion, and understanding. In the midst of this common growth they can then be life-giving to and for one another. I believe this mechanism finds its root in the common bond of faith and unconditional love that a family experiences together.

In the situation of a teenage pregnancy, it is often very valuable, with the teenager's permission, to bring the family together as a unit. The teenager can benefit immensely from the support of caring parents. It is here that feelings can be vented and shared and the family strengthened. Unfortunately, there are cases where the parents have severe problems and this ideal is an impossibility. In those cases where the young woman has decided to give birth, the family can learn that even though the sexual activity cannot be condoned, their daughter and sister is to be commended for her courage to give birth to the child rather than have an abortion. A sexual act may be a mistake. A human life never is. This speaks of a life-giving attitude that was probably rooted in the family in the first place. For this, the family should feel grateful and proud. The Bible condemns fornication, not pregnancy.

A by-product of such an approach could well be a common understanding of each member of the family unit toward the unborn child as *already* a part of the family. When such an attitude is more a thought than a reality, a young girl often does not sufficiently see the sacredness of her own life. A negative self-image, rejection experiences, feelings of worthlessness, and not being understood, all leave their mark. Thus, it is painfully logical that she will have great difficulty in seeing the sacredness of the life within her, when she sees nothing sacred or special about herself. In fact, to see the child within her as sacred and beautiful, while simultaneously seeing herself as ugly and profane, is for her an emotional contradiction. The latter bears more weight in pain and in personal history. Therefore, the unborn child must go.

Throughout several years of counseling, I have come to distinguish various steps or phases of the healing process in the young girl or woman who has had an abortion and is now seeking to be healed. It is important to bear in mind, strange though it may seem, that the woman's greater anxiety may sometimes be found in her struggle to forgive herself, and only secondly, to seek God's forgiveness. Perhaps this is because she can momentarily block God out of her life, but always carries within herself the experience and memory of her own life-destructive action, as well as the emotional and psychological consequences of that action. I shall henceforth use the word "woman" to describe the female person who has had an abortion. Though in many chronological, developmental, psychological, and emotional ways the term might not be entirely accurate, I feel the pain she has been through certainly qualifies her for the title within these pages.

My hope is that, for you who read this book and have a friend or relative who has experienced the tragedy of an abortion, perhaps these words will encourage you to judge little, heal much, and understand more fully. If it is you who are in need of that healing, may that hope all the more become a reality for you.

This book is written for the woman who has had an abortion, that she might better understand some of the intense emotions and feelings she has felt and that she may yet feel as she cries to be whole. It is also written for her friend or counsellor who cares enough to enter the healing process with her, and all those whose lives have been touched by an abortion.

Our life is so precious in the Lord's eyes, yet sometimes so worthless in our own. May His healing restore us to Him and to ourselves.

1. Perspectives

Congressman Christopher Smith (R - N.J.) once spoke about the adversary of today being the champion of tomorrow. I, too, feel that many pro-abortion and pro-choice advocates are beginning the journey of questioning and seeking to understand the pro-life position in their own minds and hearts. If the Lord is going to use us as the vehicle to bring a pro-life perspective on life, we cannot afford the luxury of judgmentalism, rashness, and vile rhetoric. Condemnation of an action without compassion for the person involved accomplishes little. We are called to cooperate with the Lord's inviting grace, to set the stage for a later conversion that, by the grace of God, might be. Nobody condemned, persecuted, or shed more blood in the early Christian community than Saul. Yet once his heart was changed, all that energy, all that motivation, and all that power was transformed into proclaiming the Christ he had formerly given so much of his life's energy to destroying. Some of the most eloquent pro-life speakers are women who have been victimized by an abortion and have been healed. They know first-hand the degradation and the exploitation. The exploitation can come from many sources.

It is crucial that these women not be exploited again by the pro-life movement. This can happen when a woman is encouraged to publicly share the story of her abortion before she is reasonably healed, and before she has had the opportunity to share that same story privately with her family, loved ones, and friends.

Also, this can happen when a woman who has had an abortion wishes to make a pro-life commitment. She is led to believe that the only way she can do it is through a rigid and judgmental attitude that demands she condemn her broken sisters as she once was condemned. How foolish, how unproductive. But more than that, how un-Christian. Judgmentalism from one who claims to have been healed is often a sign that the healing was never real or complete in the first place. Healing bears the fruit of compassion, not condemnation.

Many abortions happen each year because women feel they have no alternatives and/or support systems. That's not to say none are available. Birthright and many other organizations provide excellent services. Yet, for one reason or another, the connection may not be made. The child has been lost and often the woman regrets it almost immediately thereafter.

In terms of the pro-life position, I regret to say that even if the laws allowing abortion were changed tomorrow, there would still be many problems. We would be inundated with tremendous numbers of women seeking healing and therapy from thousands of counsellors, therapists, psychologists, and psychiatrists who saw nothing wrong with the abortion in the first place. These women would be seeking wholeness through professionals and counsellors who don't really understand, let alone believe in, the reality and dimensions of the brokenness. To heal the wrongness and pain of abortion, one must first understand that abortion is wrong and painful. As is the case even now, their pain would either be patronized or discounted. Neither are pleasant options.

Project Rachel is a priest and professional counsellor oriented ministry in Milwaukee, Wisconsin which provides professionals to help women deal with their abortions. WEBA (Women Exploited by Abortion) is an organization of support groups consisting of women who have had abortions. These are but two examples of counseling support systems that *must* be supported and expanded throughout our country. They are concrete expressions of the "Healing Centers" that are so desperately needed. Through these "centers" the woman is put in touch with her *need* for healing, by those who have been through similar pain, and then given a strong support system to respond to that need.

The women I've counseled have taught me how to lead a woman through an abortion healing process. Also, they have shown me the need for the establishment of many other forums and contacts between women who have been reasonably healed of their abortions and clergypersons, counsellors, etc. These women are the true teachers. We must learn from them, to help them. Is this not what God the Father did for us through Jesus? He became one of us to heal us and save us.

> . . . he emptied himself and took
> the form of a slave, being born in
> the likeness of man. (Phil.2:7)

The alternative is not attractive, for
history teaches us that unhealed people
have a tremendous potential for
destruction of self and others. The pain
must go somewhere, if not inward in
depression, then outward in anger. At
least, anger can help initiate the healing
process.

Psychology and therapy can do much to
assist the healing process, but ultimately
it is God's domain who shares His healing
gift, that a woman might forgive herself
and accept God's forgiveness. When
psychological insight is interwoven with a
healing ministry, two worlds converge to
offer the best. Of itself, psychology can only
help a woman understand the past and
cope with it, and that is not enough.
Knowing the "hows" and "whys" of the past
do not liberate a person from the shackles
of repetition and the reliving of the
continuous pain of the past. Forgiveness
does. That is not an invention of

humankind, but a gift of God. Spiritual healing is God's seal on the human heart that the past may not just be coped with but healed.

Ironically enough the liberation that healing brings involves a process demanding a remembrance of the past, so it may be understood and interpreted in a new way. To forget the past too soon, in an effort to bury it beyond memory, is most certainly to risk the inevitability of its reappearing in later life in an even more frightening and painful way. The effort to try and forget is all too human. We wish to block out the ugly and the violent, as well as everything and anyone connected with it.

In a healing ministry, we must seek to lead a woman who has had an abortion to remember . . . not to intensify her pain . . . but to teach her how to deal with it, that she might begin the process of letting go of her pain, and grow from it. As a woman embarks upon this journey of healing, the first gift she will receive is not instant relief, but a sense of hope . . . that healing is possible for *her*. One day she will be able to more freely forgive others because she has experienced forgiveness herself. Those others might be the parents who suggested the abortion, a boyfriend who paid for it, and even a friend who still cannot understand or deal with it.

Hope is the light at the end of the tunnel that beckons her to accept the invitation, to say yes to the urge to believe in a loving God who calls her to be whole. This is a God who wants her to know it is possible in spite of the countless sleepless nights and hidden dark fears. Her darkest hour may come right before the dawn. Help her have hope.

Needless to say, this all presupposes that the woman is in touch, or at least is beginning to get in touch, with the spark of the spiritual within herself. No one can force her to do this if she chooses not to, or if she has built up thick walls to prevent it from happening. I have met countless women who are in no way ready to face their spiritual side, either out of ignorance or fear. They will often deny the abortion bothers them, yet in the next breath they speak of sleepless nights, loss of appetite, negative self-esteem, and even an ongoing irritability and uneasiness around friends that were formerly comfortable and enjoyable companions. Perhaps even more significant are those shared ambivalent feelings of resentment and/or envy about the birth of a new baby to a friend or relative and a heightening uneasiness in the presence of infants or in conversations about them. All these signs speak of the submerged guilt and depression that often lies beneath the surface of an unhealed life. Denial is the common experience of one who has not yet committed herself to a healing process or even admitted its need. Anger and depression may also precede or even coincide with the process.

Mother Teresa of Calcutta once pointed out that there are two deaths in an abortion: the death of the unborn child *and* the death of the woman's conscience. Others, including Vicky Thorn, of *Project Rachael,* would say that it is the woman's spirit that has died and that the conscience will be later awakened as she comes to grips with the need for the healing process. Be that as it may, it is understandable that the healing process must strive not only to restore the woman to herself and reconcile her with God, here and now, but also help revive and refashion her vision of right and wrong and the spiritual courage and faith she must draw from to live out that vision (i.e. conscience). This necessarily involves the resetting of priorities and commitment to see God's human creation as especially sacred, made in His image and likeness. To destroy the most sacred expression and gift of God's creative life is in reality to lash out at the Creator Himself, by refusing His gift. The individual who does this, however, must be understood so we might help her to understand.

Saint Augustine once wrote, "I think there is a difference between one who is weak (that is, not strong) and one who is ill. . . ." Ironically enough, he wrote these words about pastors. I, too, think there is a difference between the woman who is weak . . . choosing an abortion after feeling overwhelmed by the pressures, opinions, fears of loneliness, and confusion whirling around her; and the woman who is ill . . . spiritually sick and choosing an abortion for purely selfish motives, momentarily dominated or otherwise. I believe most women who have abortions are much more weak, than ill. Both are sinful, but for the "ill woman" the abortion is much more intrinsic to her total personality and way of life, selfish and self-centered. Unfortunately, the result is the same — the unborn child dies. We give thanks that God can, and does, heal both types of women. Understanding the spiritual status, or departure point of each woman, however, does give us insight for our healing approach. We can learn, reasonably well, when her "conscience or spirit died," and the strength we must pray for to help revive it.

To many people today, abortion means money, exploitation, and power. To many others, including the woman who has chosen an abortion out of weakness, it means unbearable pain and guilt as the aftermath of an impulsive or even thought-out decision.

I do not write of this distinction to excuse either type of woman for her action. I write of it to help us understand that the journey of healing for the "weak woman" may not be quite as long as for the "ill woman." In fact, we who seek to be healers may never meet many of the latter, as they often spend much of their life's energies avoiding the reality and pain of their abortions, but, unfortunately, also the healing. Pain must be faced before it can be healed.

Perhaps from time to time we may be

fortunate enough to be sought out for support and counsel by a woman struggling with the dilemma of an unexpected or unwanted pregancy. First of all we can be aware of the enormous pressures that may be upon her. A Biblical story can help us to focus.

In this powerful story (1 Kings 3:16-28) we find Solomon as the kingly judge of Israel, one thousand years before Christ. He is confronted by two women who both claimed a newborn child as theirs. Solomon listened to their stories and then decreed, "Get me a sword . . . cut the living child in two, and give half to one woman and half to the other." The woman whose son it was, in the anguish she felt for it, said to the king, "Please my lord, give her the living child. Please do not kill it!" However, the other said, "It shall be neither mine nor yours. Divide it!" The king answered, "Give the first one the living child! By no means kill it, for she is the mother!"

In a world three thousand years later, a woman many times hears the same selfish cry and shrill advice from those around her: If you can't have the child, destroy it! In a late twentieth century society, we are led by many to believe that it is better to destroy the child we feel we cannot raise. "Abort, don't adopt! It's less painful." Our healing voice, even as an outnumbered cry in the wilderness of so many voices, is an important cry for life. We need not patronize the options to abortion as simplistic. They are not. Child-rearing and adoption are difficult. Yet, as we encounter the woman who is in the midst of a decision, we can gently, and honestly, make her aware of a world that strives to reverse the "Solomon principle." We can help her see that, in the Solomon story, the true mother who felt anguish for her child about to be destroyed is not unlike the woman of today *who does feel* great anguish after her child has been destroyed. We can help her avoid *that* anguish in a decision for the life of her unborn child and a commitment to help her in the days ahead.

Aspects of the Healing Process

The woman who has had an abortion may need to be healed of many things:

— the anger and perhaps even hatred towards those who

encouraged her to have the abortion

— the memories of the violent abortion procedure itself

— the medical personnel and others who profited by her abortion

— her child that was killed

— the grief and pain brought to others because of the abortion (e.g. boyfriend or spouse, grandparents, other children, friends, etc.)

— the death of her conscience and/or spirit when the instinct and cry for life went unheeded

The above are but descriptive words. There are many stories at the root of such words. One now follows.

"When I was sixteen I found out that I was pregnant by a thirty year old married man. I didn't find out he was married until I was too much in love with him to care. When my parents found out I was dating this man, they became furious with me. We

Condemnation of an action without
compassion for the person involved
accomplishes little.

had a terrible fight which left us, although living together, a great distance apart. Months had passed when I found that I was carrying a child. A child that was pure, beautiful, and most of all, innocent, and a child that this man didn't want any part of, and I didn't have the strength within myself to give birth to. I felt as if the only one I could depend on was the man I had already given up friends and family for. So who else could I go to? I didn't trust my parents. They'd throw me out, and then where would I go? Friends couldn't help, the ones I had left, so why tell them? Counsellors only convinced me that I was doing the right thing for me and for the baby. But probably worst of all, I didn't trust in God, who had given me the privilege of caring for one of His children, a child that was innocent, that I gave a sentence to die. I had an abortion two months into my pregnancy. It was and still is the most horrible experience I have ever had. I don't say this lightly, because physically I have been through a lot. I have been through several operations . . . and none of that has had the effect on me like killing my child has. I can't find another way to put it. In my mind there are no gentle words for the act. I still remember the day they put me on the table, bright lights were shining down on me. I laid there and prayed to the Blessed Mother Mary to understand and help me through this. I heard the machine turn on, the loud, horrible noise. And then I felt a pulling from the inside, almost as if my child were clinging to my womb for protection from this horrible machine that was taking its life. When it was over, I felt physically and mentally ill. I went through a period of time that I would wake up in a cold sweat hearing a child, my baby crying. I had horrible nightmares which could only be diluted with alcohol. Now I am twenty-four. It was eight years ago that I had an abortion and I still feel remorse and self-dislike when I look at a child or a pregnant woman. The sad part of all this is, I could have had a lot of support. I recently told my parents because I couldn't deal with it alone any more, and they have forgiven me and are trying to help with what they can right now. I still live with them, and if I would have told them, I would be living here with my child. I am presently seeing a psychiatrist and trying to understand why I didn't try harder then. I prayed to God to help me find the right words for this letter. These may seem like just words on paper to you, but it's been very real for me. But if only one person can gain something from this letter, then maybe they won't be wondering if their baby was a girl or a boy, and what he or she would look like at the age of eight."

My friend's letter is one of millions, yet it represents the words, the tears, the brokenness, and the pain of thousands. The cry: for healing and wholeness. The need: to understand the process that helps it happen. There are occasions in human history when God intervenes directly and immediately to help people. Those occasions are exhilarating yet I also think they are much less common than the gradual day-by-day, step-by-step healings. The real test is found in the "staying power." Does the changed lifestyle, deep faith, and a personal relationship with the Lord remain after the spiritual "high" has worn off? It's easy to believe on Tabor. Can one still keep the faith when it is tested in Jerusalem? I believe that for most people, healing takes place more commonly over a period of months, sometimes years. It is that process these women have taught me through their stories and experiences that I would like to share with you. I feel they have educated me through their honesty and trust, as well as their pain and guilt. The words that follow represent their stories.

In no way do I intend to minimize or underrate the role of psychiatrists, psychologists, or counsellors. In fact, very often when a psychiatrist has been working for a period of time with a woman who has had an abortion, he or she will ask me to join them for a session so I might get to know the woman and establish a degree of trust. After the session, the trust relationship continues to build and at the appropriate time, when the woman is ready and longing to celebrate the healing she's experiencing, we'll celebrate the Sacrament of Reconciliation. In the Catholic tradition, the Sacrament of Reconciliation is an expression and a celebration of a healing process that is already in motion. Healing happens not only when the woman reaches up and out, but when she grasps God's hand as He reaches down. God's grace has been working long before the woman seeks out a priest to absolve her, that she might be reconciled with her loving Father and with Jesus' Body, the community of the church.

Both suffer when a life is lost. A sense of appropriate timing must be respected or the sacrament may mean little to the woman. We must appreciate the woman's need to "feel" healed. Please understand, I am not relegating the Sacramental Reconciliation to a spiritual "high." Yet without the solid substance of pastoral sensitivity and a sense of the woman's timing to be healed, she will perceive herself to be the subject of a mechanical spiritual process, rather than the recipient of her divine Father's deep love, following a personal encounter with her God. The experience and acceptance of healing flows from a real and trusting relationship with Christ, His church, and His minister. A brief and sometimes all too rigid ritual is not enough. "Ex opere operato" (forgiveness from the action of the sacrament alone) may make theological sense to many, but it's often irrelevant and meaningless to the wounded woman.

The trust relationship is the foundation of the healing process. It would be a mistake to believe that initially, trust is easily given without being earned. The woman who has had an abortion is cautious, and perhaps inclined to be untrusting, and reasonably so. Very possibly the people she trusted the most in this world, parents, friends, and even clergymen or clergywomen, were the very ones who strongly urged and advised her to have the abortion: "It's the best thing." "It'll solve your problem." Now she knows differently. If her advisors were not consciously lying, even if they really believed that abortion was the the best choice, they were wrong. The principle pain that remains is now hers. Sincerity was not enough, truth and the facts were needed. Now she's not sure who to trust. The gift of trust must be earned by he or she who will receive it.

It's important to remember, that one comes to know a woman who has had an abortion; not an aborted woman. This is very important. In other situations, one may minister to a person who is old, not an old person. One talks to a person who is blind, not a "blind person." I once walked into a house and the little three year old, Billy, came in. "Hi, Billy. This is Father Mike." "Hi, priest!" shouted Billy, and later, "Bye, priest." He could only understand me in terms of the images his parents presented. Their perspectives

36

became his. If the perspective is distorted, the uniqueness of personhood and individuality is diminished and stereotypes will take over. One will see too much of the abortion and not enough of the person of the woman, too much of the action and not enough of the person behind the action. I'll know it happened, but won't be open enough to understand where it came from. Not only histories of civilizations, but personal histories as well are destined to be repeated if we do not learn the lessons from them.

Reflections

1. What are your feelings about listening to a woman tell her personal story about having an abortion?

2. What would be or has been your reaction when an acquaintance or close friend has told you privately about her abortion?

3. "We must learn from them to help them." Do you welcome this advice or resent it?

4. Do you feel a healing attitude towards a woman who has had an abortion "waters down" the seriousness of her action?

5. "Pain must be faced before it can be healed." How do you personally feel about this statement?

6. What aspect of the healing process do you think is the most difficult to resolve or deal with?

7. What role do you believe God plays in the healing process?

2. Foundation of the Healing Process

In building a relationship with the person who has had an abortion, it is inevitable that she will test you to discover if she can share her story with you, if you are safe and honest. She has met many who have told her what she *wanted* to know and hear. Will you be one who she can trust, one who will tell her what she *needs* to know and hear . . . gently, yes . . . but honestly, too? If you sense that you're not the right person, do not insist otherwise. Do not force her. Do not play games. Give serious thought, reflection, and prayer to recommending her to another counsellor priest, minister, or friend who is more appropriate for her personality and her style of trust and sharing. As a part of the Lord's healing ministry, we are not called to be a woman's guru, but her friend. To really care is to wish the best for the other, and perhaps to predispose her to be open to the experience of healing that will come through one we have recommended, if not ourselves.

A woman might come with much emotional excess baggage. One woman I know came to a counsellor two years after meeting him. "I have a question," the counsellor said. "I'm confused. I've never had a conflict with you, we've never had an angry word, but for two years of seeing you in various places, I've felt hostility. I've felt anger. I've felt rejection. Help me understand where that came from." She said, "In high school, I had a teacher who put me down and hurt me badly — your height, your hair color, your mannerisms. You used to remind me of him until I learned that you are different." As trust builds, it is helpful to learn who we are in the eyes and perceptions of others so we might better help them to deal with past images and distorted comparisons. Then, we can more freely and honestly tell them who we are.

Check-Out Time

Initially, individuals are much more comfortable talking about *things* rather than themselves. As the sharing and trust relationship begins to build, it is helpful to talk about things, activities, and events happening around the woman, non-threatening and easy. Talk about things that interest her. Talk about things that do not come "too close" to her. Use an initial conversation as a tone setter, and again a way of *letting her* get to know you. This provides a very necessary check-out time. Possibly, the first session will bring only light conversation. Give her time. Let her gradually ease into the depth of sharing that will come. She may want you to take the initiative and the lead: "How about spending the first session just getting to know each other? And unless you indicate otherwise, I'm not going to push you to get into any 'heavies' today. But then the next time we get together, hopefully you'll be more comfortable with me and then we can start sharing the things that are deeper within you."

Ask her how she came to hear of you, and how she felt as she was coming in the door for the appointment. Ask her how she feels now. She may want to ask you questions about your background and interests and how you came to be involved in this ministry.

We cannot seek wholeness through
those who don't really understand or
believe in the reality of our
brokenness.

Your openness will condition and encourage her. Remember, abortion, which is the core of what you want to discuss in the sharing relationship with her, is not the center of her life. The times she has been taken advantage of sexually or emotionally, the times she thought the only thing she had to give was the sexual, the times that she was manipulated, exploited — and what she is really worth as a person — these things are at the center of her life. The abortion was the trigger on the gun. The revolver had been loaded for quite some time.

The Test

Do not be surprised if the woman tests you. Try not to be defensive. In her eyes, she may have been betrayed by one like you, or like me, before. As I said previously, we might remind her of others. A slip of the tongue, a hostile word, an appointment with her when you've already been dragging yourself through several hours of appointments and you've got to go with one more and you are very tired, any or all of these can communicate uncaring and lead to a *perceived* feeling of betrayal and rejection. The key word here is *perceived*.

In actuality, I might care very deeply, but if for some reason, through a word, a glance, an expression, the woman perceives and feels the opposite, then I must back up and help her get in touch and express *why* she feels that way. I must seek to understand the root of the perception — the specific situation, experience or discussion that led to it.

Do not be afraid to tell her how *you* feel. Be open. Tell her that you must learn about her, as a person and all that that means. She may categorize herself in your eyes as just "another problem." She is the only one who can teach you who she is. Her speed and level of self-disclosure is her gift to give. We must clearly communicate to her how special and sacred we consider that gift to be, and how privileged we feel to receive it.

We are called to lead the woman to see her status and self-definition in terms of her daughtership to the one Father, rather than in any action or mistake she's made, in *who she is* rather than in what she's done. The strength and wholeness of the former is to transform the weakness and brokenness of the latter. It means she may have to see herself in an entirely new way.

A Reason

As Father John Powell, S.J., a well
known author and lecturer from Loyola
University of Chicago, so eloquently
mentions in his book, *Abortion, the Silent
Holocaust,* many parents of handicapped
children are not able to say, "My baby has
a life not worthy to be lived," even though
many physicians feel that way. Now we
have a whole cadre of physicians and
others who who see it as their personal
crusade to help parents give "informed
consent" to the death of their child. These
physicians and others fail to see that the
child has an inherent right to life as a child
of God. His dignity is in the relationship to
the God who created him. Ironically
enough, the woman who has been
encouraged by others to see the "rightness"
of this "informed consent" thinking in
terms of her baby yesterday, is often the
woman who sees the same "rightness" of
this thinking in terms of herself today,
because she fails to see that she, like her
child, has the same inherent dignity. Thus,
frequently the woman most vulnerable to
abortion has a sense of low self-esteem, her
handicap. If she is not seen as worth much
in her own eyes, how could the child within

45

her be seen as worth any more? The destruction of her unborn child is but another side of her own self-destructive feelings. The more positive a woman feels about herself, the less likely she will be manipulated, exploited, used, or led to do something that is as intrinsically self destructive as abortion. Conversely, the less positive she feels about herself, the less she loves herself, the more vulnerable she will be to self destructive attitudes and behavior.

Be In Touch With Yourself

We must be in touch with our own values, faith, and self-image before we can try to be the Lord's instrument to help heal another. That means God is the healer and we are His instruments. In my own ministry I've often said, "As a friend I can love you. As a priest I can help to heal you." If we put ourselves in the center, "*I* had a great session, it went really well, *I* did great, she's doing good," and then the next session flounders, we put ourselves on a downward spiral. It's as if we're the coach for the team and the whole squad depends upon us for victory. In this way of thinking the woman is short-changed and we operate under illusions or delusions of grandeur. The healing process takes place in its rhythm between God and the soul of the woman. We are but conductors, instruments, and enablers. When we put ourselves in the center, the situation will become very confused and overpowering.

In many ways, we're not really free to share this kind of ministry until we've been broken ourselves. We're not really free until we've had the experience of pouring our hearts out at three o'clock in the afternoon, to learn that at seven that night the woman still went ahead and had the abortion. She might even come back the next day and say, "Now will you still give me a hug? Do you still care?" Again, we're tested. We're not really free until we give her that hug the next day and start over.

Once a woman whose friend had three or four abortions said to me, "How do you keep huggin' her? She's repulsive to me. I feel nauseous in her presence." I responded, "Maybe if someone had hugged her after the first abortion there wouldn't have been a second. Maybe if after the second, there wouldn't have been a third." The possibility of conversion and healing is always

47

present. We're called to convert, not condemn. Condemnation may destroy the seeds of conversion and healing. That doesn't mean we're playing down the abortion, pretending it wasn't significant, pretending it didn't matter. However, the woman may be convinced, as the adulterous woman in the Gospel of John (chapter eight), that her whole life is worthless, and she doesn't want to dig deeper or see any more of herself than is necessary to survive each day. She's tremendously afraid to dig because deep down she's going to find more worthlessness, more emptiness. We say, "Try! Believe! Dig! Underneath all that pain and memory find the spark of your own goodness." Our Jewish brothers and sisters call that the "ruah," the part of us deep down that makes us who we are and cries out to God for connection and relationship with Him. When our "ruah," our spirit, is linked up in rhythm with, on the same wave length as, God's Holy Ruah, Holy Spirit, then we're free, free to be ourselves, free to live God's call to become who we really were all along. We're no longer bound by the things we did, because who we are goes so far beyond what we did. We live in a functional, pragmatic world.

"What are you worth? How much do you make? Where do you live? What's the size of your car?" That's what you're worth. And we in the Christian tradition say "No" to that. Who you are, your first posture in life, is a child of God. God doesn't withhold His love. *We* interrupt it. *He* doesn't stop it. He continues to invite. His arms are open, the embrace is welcome. We have to encourage the woman to see she has the right, the possibility of the dream of walking down that aisle and embracing Christ as her brother. We have to reawaken that dormant, not dead, dream within her.

The Depth Of Goodness

A call to wholeness and healing demands the goodness felt about self from *within* is stronger than the negative pressure one feels from *without*. If ten "friends" told the woman to have the abortion, perhaps it was only one faint voice that said, "Don't." In fighting today for the life of the unborn, we're trying to reverse a societal pressure cooker and a values vacuum. We're trying to help women build a positive sense from within that is so strong it can overcome all the negativity that is programmed to her from without. We are in a sense, dealing with a counter-cultural experience, and a society that believes faith is unscientific, useless, and even superstitious. When our world sees something of faith, something or someone holy, many think it's an anomaly, something separate from reality. We put it on a shelf and gaze at it from a distance, as though it were a museum piece, to be studied and analyzed, not enjoyed and shared. In actuality, the holy is part of the whole, and the whole is integral to what reality is all about. The real world is to live the holy from within. The plastic world is the other one. We must deeply believe that ourselves, and live our lives that way, or we will be swallowed up, condemned, and made fools of for our own words and lack of commitment to them. As Christians we are called to change the world. All too often, it happens the other way around. The woman who shares her journey back to wholeness can hardly believe us if we don't believe ourselves.

The Statement and the Story

Behind every statement, there's a story. This story may well be the statement's point of origin. Healing involves responding to the story rather than reacting against the statement. "I hate blacks." "I hate whites." "I hate Hispanics." "I can't stand Vietnamese." They're all statements we've heard. We must try to learn and understand the stories that are behind the statements even if we do not agree with them. What happened? How? When? Why? Often, we go on a "head trip," an "intellectual tangent." How can we defend a group that's under attack, using ethical, spiritual, and theological arguments? Head trips don't change people. Hearts change people. One way or another, when people's hearts are opened, their heads will follow. People begin to trust us, not when they share their statements, but when they share their stories. It is then, in the midst of that trust and sharing of stories, that they're open to re-evaluate and possibly change their statements.

When I was ordained about six months (back then I had all the answers, now I'm working on the questions!), I was taking the census at a home in the parish. The door opened, and an elderly woman ushered me in. The door shut. An eighty pound dog, sixty pounds of mouth and twenty pounds of body, seemed to give that, "I'm going to have you for lunch" look. The woman then started screaming and getting angrier and angrier. The bitterness was obvious! Like a boil that was lanced, the pus kept pouring out, and I kept listening, because I was compassionate, and sensitive, (or because I was terrified that I might get nailed by that big puppy!). She started sharing her story. She was very active in the parish years ago, and was hurt by a priest — three years before I was born! She carried that hurt within her all that time. Perhaps to this day that priest may not be aware of her pain. Her healing began when I listened, not just in my name, but in the name of others who hurt her. If we can listen long enough to the statements and let those who hurt express their anger without getting defensive, they'll usually come to trust us with their stories. As we hear the story, we might even transpose it. We might say to ourselves, "If I had grown up like that woman, in that house, with those influences, in that city, with those friends, and I became pregnant, I wonder how I would have had the strength to avoid an abortion." In this, the Lord helps to keep us humble, real, and in touch.

Judgmentalism and self-righteousness,

needless to say, have no place in the healing process. The woman is not our enemy. It is our own ego. We have the spiritual power to do what we're called to do. God never calls His community to a task without gifting it with the charisms needed to accomplish it. An author once wrote, "There's no limit to the amount of good a man or woman can do if he or she doesn't care who gets the credit." The most brilliant ideas are by people, authors of whom we'll never know, because they've shared their gifts and dreams, and sought little or nothing in return other than to help others.

Another's Pain

As a woman shares her story, we understand the need to "walk in another's moccasins." First we must take off our own moccasins, our own self-righteousness, our own judgmentalism, our own hang-ups, our own "I-knew-a-girl-just-like-you-once" isms. When we take off our own moccasins, then we can put on hers, and walk a mile in them, and be as fully compassionate and understanding as God intended us to be. "There but for the grace of God go I" can be more than a trite cliche.

To forget the past too soon — in an
effort to bury it beyond memory — is
most certainly to risk the inevitability
of its reappearing in later life in an
even more frightening and painful
way.

We all have our pet peeves and convictions. Those prejudices and feelings about given actions and types of people we carry over from one stage of life to the next. God might use us as his instruments to heal the woman who has had an abortion. He also might use her to heal us of our judgments and prejudices. God waits until the end of our lives to judge us, after He's given us all possible chances and opportunities to say yes to His love. If only we could do that with each other!

Compassion — Not Condonation

Understanding and compassion for the pain and brokenness of another does not demand that we agree with the negative or sinful behavior. We must separate the two. Accept the sinner and reject the sin. The woman cries, "I cannot be healed. I'm lost, I'm no good." Jesus invites her to deep digging and digging and digging until she reaches that place of sacredness within herself. Therein lies her experience of Abba, Loving Father. Jesus leads her out of that pit of self-hatred, into liberation. The process is laid out in the gospels. It's as old as the carpenter of Nazareth, as new as the woman you met yesterday.

As alluded to in the introduction, in a world of decades gone by, parents and adults commonly felt it best to discourage the negative in the young by emphasizing the negative. Deterrence through fear was the strategy. "If you get pregnant I'll break every bone in your body!" Even this often repeated phrase was shouted in love! No doubt, many a fearful teenager has opted for abortion rather than deal with the imagined or real parental consequences.

Today, a woman who has personally known the pain of abortion can do much to deter the same decision of a friend. Deterrence is not so much instilling fear in her of what will happen from those around her, but informing her of the brokenness that will take place within her. The brokenness may come from the woman's instinctive feminine sense that something special and alive has been destroyed, or from explicitly that the life destroyed was God's gift, created in His image, and that gift was refused and destroyed.

Speaking The Truth

Your commitment to be a "truth-speaker" in the life of the woman who has had an abortion can help her greatly. Being a "truth-speaker" helps call you to share what she *needs* to hear, rather than what she might *want* to hear. It is a call on your part to trust her with the truth. Father Richard Rohr, O.F.M., founder of the *New Jerusalem Community* in Cincinnati, Ohio, often speaks of this theme. Never use truth as a weapon. The way one makes a point is just as important as the point itself. When the woman completes or brings to some kind of closure the healing process in her own life, and spiritually begins to be integrated back into the faith community, we might be tempted to say to ourselves, "Wow, this is great. Now when she sees me at church, she'll give me a big hug. When she comes up to Communion, I'll get a big smile. When she sees me in the store, I'll get a big Hi!" Then you notice: "She's avoiding me at church, goes to another Communion line, and doesn't come near me in the store." She brought a reasonable closure to the pain and in her own mind might have had a need to bring closure to all aspects surrounding it. That might include her relationship with the one who helped heal her. In a sense, she might need to forget about me to move on with her life. Here we're right back to the ego question again. If we're hung up on ego or how we look or appear in the eyes of others, we'll be led astray. When a woman is healed and comes back to say things, it's a special memory, but we must not expect it or be emotionally dependent on it. To do so is to have less to offer to the woman who needs us next. That which we have received as a gift, we must give as a gift. If she ever does something to hurt us, we must never violate the confidentiality. This can be a problem, especially in support groups. People may be warm and friendly one week, and the next week be dealing with deeper pains and momentarily coping by withdrawing or even lashing out at those new-found friends. Instead of understanding the pain and riding it out, they may violate the confidentiality, and obstruct the whole continuation of the healing process. Support groups can be tremendously helpful and therapeutic for people, yet one week to another may bring highs and lows, with Tabors and Gethsemanes, all wrapped up together. When confidentiality is violated, trust is destroyed.

Reflections

1. How do you feel when you're "tested for trust?" Resentful? Understanding? Turned off?

2. "If she herself is not seen as worth much in her own eyes, how could the child within her be seen as worth any more?" How would you begin to address this attitude in a friend who came to you for help?

3. "We're called to convert, not condemn." What is the main characteristic or tendency in your personality that would: 1) enhance conversion 2) make you prone to condemnation?

4. Recall an experience from your past when you first heard the statement and then listened further and compassionately for the story. What was the result?

5. Does your ego ever get in the way of the potential good you can do? When? How?

6. Do you ever feel you're walking a tightrope between compassion and condonation? How do you handle it? Are you comfortable and satisfied with the way you handle it? Why or why not?

3. Friendship

Friendship

They never knew! My parents never knew. I mean, how could I tell my parents that their "little girl" had lost her virginity at 15 years old. After all, I was the one they expected to go to college, to make "something" of my life.

Besides, it was the first time I had ever made love. Now I had missed my third period and my mother was starting to ask questions. I had to do something!

My boyfriend didn't know what to do, either, so we talked to one of his teachers. She gave me the number of Planned Parenthood and told me to call right away.

They gave me an appointment right away. After going through the necessary exams, tests, etc. they sent me upstairs to a nice grey-haired lady.

She said, "Your tests show you are

probably 14 weeks. What do *you* want to do?"

"I don't know. I'm only 15 years old and my parents would kill me if they found out that I was pregnant!"

She gave me the number of the abortion clinic. She even let me call on her phone! They made the appointment for the following week.

She warned me it might be a little more expensive because I was already 14 weeks and they could do up to 12 weeks with no problems.

My boyfriend cried. "Couldn't we just get married and have the baby?"

"Please don't cry! I just can't! They'd hate me."

So he took me anyway. My sister came to support me. We were very close. We walked up to the front door. I remember thinking that abortion was dirty, but this office was really nice. "It must be okay," I reasoned.

One girl sat next to me and asked if it was my first time. "Yes," I said, "And you?" "Oh," she exclaimed, "this is my third time."

Then a nicely dressed woman took me in a room and explained the procedure. Of course there was no mention of *baby,* only "tissue." With gentle gestures she demonstrated how the doctor would remove "the tissue" with the suction tube.

The time came. I signed my release and paid my $275.00 cash and was led downstairs. I was instructed to undress and put on a hospital gown. I got on the table and put my feet in the stirrups. They asked me if I wanted sodium pentothal or ether. I chose the sodium pentothal. "Count back from 100," she said and smiled.

I remember thinking what are they going to do with it? There was a stainless steel bowl with stuff in it but I thought it must be iodine or something. Oh well, 98, 97 . . . I was out.

I woke up, back in my stall, where I was told to get up, it was time to leave. They gave me some Darvon for the pain and I left.

I cried all the way home. I don't know why, I just couldn't control my tears. (To this day I can't even listen to the same music he played on the tape deck as it brings back all the details.)

Within two years we had broken off our

relationship. This really put a strain between us.

My sister asked me if I felt guilt. "No," I said, "What for?"

But years later the guilt came, and the pain and the remorse, but I kept denying it as I drank another drink. Drugs and alcohol really numbed the pain. I never consciously thought of why, just that it made the hurt go away.

I met a man and dated him for four years. Then I found out I was pregnant. I was ready to break off the relationship before I found out I was pregnant. This time I knew I couldn't go through an abortion again. So we got married.

I almost died the first time I read a detailed description of a 16 week old "baby." That's when I first broke down and cried. That's when I realized that "it" was a baby. I don't think I've stopped crying since.

Even harder to accept is that the man I married has a son from his previous marriage who was born the same week as mine would have been.

I learned of Jesus' love and forgiveness

two years ago. It was the first time in over eight years that I've had any peace.

I still lapse into feeling guilty at times but I search during those times for a closer walk with God, and He is faithful as He gives me peace.

I thank God I was in your workshop. You let me know it's okay to grieve for my little one. She was my child and I can go ahead and cry for my loss.

Now I accept her as my first child — "the baby I'll never hold."

"If I knew then what I know now, you never would have died!"

Clearly, then, healing is a process that takes time unique to each person and individual. The steps and time must be respected. If we rush, or omit one of these steps, problems will develop later from unresolved feelings. In some way, shape, manner, or form, the woman will go back and reexperience unresolved guilt or hurts that will have to be addressed then, because that step was avoided earlier. This can happen if we are too much in a hurry or even uncomfortable with the content of her guilt.

In ministering to women who suffered through a rape or abortion, I used to say, "Yes, this is very personal, intimate, and I don't want to get into the details of the actual abortion. I don't want to go too deep into the details of the actual rape situation." I didn't want to intensify the woman's pain. Thus, I would skim over the experience, respecting, what I thought was her uncomfortableness. Often, I found that the woman would come back to me some time later and say, "I need to talk about that. Now will you listen to the whole story?" Though I thought I was being compassionate to her by not digging too deep, she had a need to say more, express more, that she might better confront, deal with, and resolve her own feelings. She was saying, "If I didn't trust you, I wouldn't have picked you to talk to." This does not mean that we should pry excessively, but the point is, it makes a great deal of sense when we realize the extent of personal sacrifice to which a woman will go in search of her healing. When someone calls from two hundred miles away, and drives those miles to talk to you, she's ready to talk! I find it helpful to say, as mentioned in chapter 1, "Spend the first session checking me out from my 'gums to my toenails!' Ask me any questions you wish and resolve any doubts or apprehensions you might have about me and where I'm coming from, and why I'm here for you. We can't afford to play games. The world's been playing games with you too long. Once the cards are on the table, if you really trust me and can look in my eyes and tell me that, then, I'm going to ask you whatever I think is appropriate, whatever I feel you need to share to help this healing process."

A Listening Heart

Counsellors often speak of the importance of listening with the heart, not just the head — to what's being said, and to what's not being said. If there are four chairs in the room, does the woman sit in the one farthest away? If you move your chair three inches closer, do you see her leaning back in hers? Does she look out the window as she talks to you, or is she able to hold eye contact? Is her body posture and position relaxed or tense? Do you pick up other signs and signals? Does she need a couple of moments of escape from you? If so, you can offer to get her something to drink, or go outside the room so she has

Denial is the common experience of
one who has not yet committed
herself to the healing process or even
admitted its need.
Pain must be faced before it can be healed.

three or four minutes to take a deep breath and compose herself if she is particularly nervous. Look for the body language signals. She'll send them to you loud and clear in her own way. Once you get to know her and as the session draws to an end, affirm her and say, "I feel you're much more relaxed." Specifically, she may ask, "How do you know that?" "Well, remember when you first walked in and then almost walked out a minute later? I can see that you're much more at ease now." She might well laugh, "Yeah, I was really nervous!" Then you can break through another barrier by laughing about where she was, compared to where she is, and the growth that has taken place in such a short period of time. Some of these words may sound like common sense to you. Yet to the woman before us, they might be tremendously important, for she may be coming to us after debating with herself about doing so for a long period of time. Even then, she may feel very anxious about talking with us.

This is not a process one follows through to completion when all is wrapped up in a neat and tidy package. It is a step-by-step struggle. When the woman takes a step forward, makes an inch of progress, we should affirm her vigorously. Tie that "walk" in with your own faith. If the woman is Catholic, you're leading her towards a reconciliation sacramentally with the Lord and with His Body, the church community. If she's not Catholic, we're still leading her towards that reconciliation within the tradition and convictions that are hers. Process the journey of healing each moment of the way. "I have a sense that God is really smiling on you today and is really proud of you. You drove here, you came here, you're trusting. It really tells me how humble I should be, that of all the people God could have chosen for you to share your story with, God chose me." It's important that we feel and believe that. Many faithfilled and beautiful things happen when a woman goes literally miles out of her way to seek *you* out. When she picks you, you're special. These women sense a gift in us. Seek not to relate to her with anyone's style but your own. Do it in your own style, with your own God-given personality, uniqueness, and gifts, using these insights to help. The most valuable instrument of healing the Lord has given her is the person of *you*.

A Holy Person

Commit yourself to be a holy person to your friend. Perhaps this woman came to you as a stranger. By now you should see each other as friends. It is not just she who is sharing herself with you, it is you as well, sharing with her. Out of that comes a sense of the sacred. As Father Vincent Dwyer says, a holy person is someone in whose presence I feel sacred about myself. The more comfortable, trusting, and open she becomes with you, the deeper the friendship. A positive friendship is transformed into spiritual intimacy when she is led to look beyond you and see the person of Christ in you, when she sees God seeing her as you see her, when the sacredness she feels she possesses in God's eyes is reflected in the sacredness she feels in your eyes. This is a profound experience, but there is also a place for a sense of humor. Some words may come out in tears one moment and laughter the next, especially as the tragic irony becomes evident. It may seem crazy at first, but remember, laughter is a release too. If the woman in the midst of her healing tragedy process can find a moment of laughter, accept it as therapeutic, for it really is. As

We must appreciate the woman's
need to "feel" healed.
The woman herself is the only one
who can teach you who she is.

for the tears, I've heard and long believed that we'll often remember those we've laughed with, but never forget those we've cried with.

What is the place of guilt in all this? I've spoken to some who feel it is a totally negative and useless feeling. Others believe it is an important component of religious growth.

I see guilt as healthy and productive when it leads the woman to come to grips with the reality of what she has done. It can be a part of the way back to wholeness and inner peace through a personal relationship with a loving and forgiving God, and a commitment to embark upon the journey of that relationship. Once this "commitment to healing" process is set in motion, there is no value in guilt whatsoever. It would only obstruct rather than conduct the Lord's healing power and the woman's faith growth. Peter could not afford the "luxury of guilt" for his sin of denial on that Holy Thursday night, for Jesus had much more he wanted him to do for a new-born church community.

That is not to say many did not benefit from the story of Peter's denial, the Lord's forgiveness, and the profound sense of compassion that a forgiven Peter must have had for others. It is to say Peter was not burdened when he told his story, but liberated in gratefulness and faith.

Likewise, once a woman who has had an abortion begins the journey of healing, guilt has no place. Faith is the call.

Reflections

1. How do you feel when someone trusts you deeply? Unworthy? Scared? Proud?

2. What do you do, or say, in your own style, to help put another at ease who's beginning to trust you?

3. Recall a time in your life when another made you feel sacred and special. How did that affect your life? Your relationship with God?

4. Recall a time in your life when you made another feel sacred or special. How did that affect the other person's life? His or her relationship with God?

5. Do you believe guilt has any role to play in the healing process?

4. The Steps of Reconciliation

1. In Touch with the Past

Memories to this point may have been preludes to more pain. The experience of healing is a time of reconciliation, the time for the woman to grow in her "yes" to the gift of God's forgiving love. This can be very difficult. Taking God seriously in his invitation to be forgiven, absolved, healed, and made whole is an awesome challenge. Many women, for a long time, think it to be impossible. "How can God forgive me after all I've done?"

As Ila Ryan, a victim of four abortions, of the Maryland Chapter of *WEBA,* recalls in her story, "Relief immediately follows abortion. The problems are solved. 'No one knows' is the thought. Then the haunting realization: God knows. I know. I can't take it to Him, though. He could never forgive me! I'll take it to the bottle, the pill. I'll take it back to the sexual. I'll have another baby (called an atonement baby by many) to replace the one/s I've lost. That will make me feel better!"

Before abortion-reconciliation is a question of forgiveness, it is a question of faith. It is what I often call the "Judas-Peter syndrome." In a sense, Peter's sin was greater than Judas'. They were both betrayals but Peter's was a thrice betrayal and he was the leader of the community Jesus founded. Judas' betrayal set a chain of events in motion that led to the crucifixion of Jesus. What enabled Peter to overcome the guilt and devastation and go on to lead the community once again? What prevented Judas from forgiving himself and starting over? What led him to destroy himself, even though he, as Peter, had personally known the same loving Jesus for three years? Very simply, Peter truly *believed* that Jesus was Messiah, Lord, and Savior "enough" to forgive him. He *believed* Jesus' love was stronger than any sin he could commit, and it was. Thus, in faith, Peter went to Jesus and was forgiven. The forgiveness led not just to Peter's reinstatement in the community but Jesus' admonition to do even more. Peter knew the need for compassion in ministry first-hand. Perhaps of all the apostles, he was the most powerful recipient.

Judas, on the other hand, could not fathom Jesus forgiving him. His sin was too "evil" even for Jesus to forgive. The result was despair. (Remember, unhealed people have a tremendous capacity for self-destruction.) The consequence was suicide. "To destroy my pain I must destroy me!" is the cry.

How much pain, guilt, and grief we could spare ourselves if we learned to take God's love seriously! Someone once wrote: "God helps those who stop hurting themselves." How true.

When the immediate relief after the abortion wears off, faith guidance is desperately needed. A balance is important. We strive to help the woman get in touch with the past, not to be overwhelmed by it, but to deal with it through the eyes of faith. We hope to allow and help the woman to get in touch with the specific situations that caused or led to the pain and hurt of the abortion. What kind of relationships, what kind of prior stereotypes, images (about manhood, womanhood, masculinity, femininity,

If the woman sees herself as not worth much, how can she see the child within her as worth any more?

sexuality, personhood, self-image) led to the pain from which the abortion was to provide escape? "Well, when I was ten years old. . . ." Many times the woman has been through some kind of a sexual abuse situation that led her to a vulnerable, distorted perception of self, and then to sexual activity and abortion. As we said before, the lower the self image, the greater the possibility of manipulation and exploitation. The woman who believes she is worth very little will expend little energy to defend that all too low self-image. Anger turned inward *is* depression. The woman who has finally been able to get in touch with her feelings and the anger within may find herself momentarily screaming and shouting and even using a few choice words. Let her do it. The anger is much healthier than depression.

If we're tempted to be judgmental with her and question her faith, we can read Jeremiah (20:14-18). He not only made excuses to God when he was called to be a prophet, he cursed the day he was born. He even cursed the man that ran though the village to bring his father the news of his birth. And yet, he believed, somehow, that God's will would triumph — through him!

79

Finally, he was murdered by his own countrymen, at the very hands of those the Lord called to receive his prophetic message.

If she screams at us, she may be screaming at God, and to her, we represent Him. At first the situation may take us back a little bit. We may be tempted to become a little resentful. Try very hard not to be. Stand by her. Abortion is the action of a lonely person, who often considers it the only option. Healing is the cry of that same lonely person who can be shown a way back. Through this, too, the trust will build.

There may be the danger to be "over-compassionate," and minimize the gravity of the situation. A life has been lost. A child has been destroyed. We don't make excuses for her mistake or decision. We try to understand it, but not rationalize it. "Oh, it's okay. You didn't know what you were doing." Maybe morally, conscience-wise, even theologically, that could be true. Only God knows that. Judgment is left to Him. To give her a cop-out, an escape from dealing with the reality of what she has done will not help her. The reality of what she has done must be named and understood if true reconciliation is to take place. Let her continue to deal with the anger and work it through. Even with the best of intentions, we musn't frustrate the healing process by feeling so much compassion for her, that we by-pass or cut short feelings that must be felt and dealt with. We won't be helping her. The whole healing process will be frustrated. We seek to confront and conquer the past, not avoid it. The goal is to help this woman, a friend, to cope. She might have been in a "better-living-through-chemistry" lifestyle, and abusing drugs frequently. "I can't deal with it, so I'll go out and hurt a guy." I once asked a woman who was very sexually active, "Don't you feel you're being used by those men?" "No way, I'm using them!" was her reply. That was her perception. She would park along the highway with a C.B. radio, navigating business prospects. (I used to get a lot of looks when she'd come to the rectory. She was usually dressed in her work clothes!)

2. Healing: God's Realm

Remind your friend throughout the sessions to see that as a friend, you can love and accept her, but healing is the Lord's domain. The author of life is He who must heal the loss of life. True, healing always comes from another. The woman may get uptight and utter, "You know, I've been with you three sessions now and I don't feel better about it. I don't feel good. I came here so *you'd* make me feel good." Put the focus back on God's healing process, and *His time*. We're not her God. We can't let her substitute one level of emotional dependency for another. We can't let her substitute one "cult figure" for another. Her boyfriend is now no good, and now we're her new savior? Don't get trapped into that.

The God image in this, needless to say, is crucial. We may even have to be sensitive to her reaction when we talk to her about a loving Father. Was she ever hurt deeply or even molested by her father? Certainly God is our loving Father, and Jesus our loving brother no matter what. But it still might be necessary to help her redefine and give new meaning to those words, because of her past experiences of them.

It is even possible that a woman's poor image of her father may be a factor in her decision to have an abortion. The abortion, even subconsciously, may be one way of denying her father's power over her and her feelings of powerlessness while living at home or within her father's grasp. The destruction of the unborn child is one way to strike back, especially if the child is seen as important to the father and an expression of his power.

On the other hand, the father of the aborted baby may be hurting deeply over the loss of his child too — a child he might have desperately wanted to be born. If this is so, grieving will be no stranger to him either, and his healing process may be very similar to his former or present partner's, the mother of the baby. Much more attention, emotional and spiritual support should be given to the grieving fathers, though at present they come forward for help much less frequently.

A final word about the God image. Some might say that the healing process would be better facilitated by changing the God-head titles. We must remember, however, that Father, Son, and Holy Spirit refer not only to roles but to relationships within the Trinity. Healing more genuinely takes place in the life of the woman when she is able to honestly redefine Father and

Condemnation may destroy the seeds
of conversion and healing.
The woman who believes she is
worth very little will expend little
energy to defend that all too low self
image.

even Son, if necessary, as positive, rather than deny or change their titles. Then she can relate to them in a positive, mutual, and loving way as she comes to share in God's very life. If we simply change the names of the persons of the Trinity, she may miss the opportunity to be healed in the fullest possible way. The words of Donald G. Bloesch, from his book, *The Battle for the Trinity,* can add further theological clarification: "It is important to understand that it is not we who name God, but it is God who names Himself by showing us who He is!"

Accepting Healing

What was it that allowed the Peter we spoke of, to even seek reconciliation, be healed, and internalize that brokenness that it might be a new strength to give glory to God in the ministry of the newborn church? Peter was a living example of 2 Corinthians 12:9. "My grace is enough for you. In (your) weakness (my) power reaches perfection." The Peter that believed Jesus' embrace was large enough to heal his three mistakes is the Peter our friend can draw strength from as well.

We can easily slip into the use of ample Bible quotes. But beyond that there is a need to communicate the spiritual reality and fact behind the Scripture stories and verses: God can and does *want* to heal. There is a part of God that will touch her, and we must help it come to her in the way she needs it, instead of in the way we want it to happen. Faith, in a loving God, is the basis and the core of the healing, and I believe it has two parts. A little story can illustrate my point. A couple of years ago, a seventeen year old girl came in for a session. We had never met before. She came on the recommendation of a friend. She sat down and began to tell me that she was struggling with the whole area of homosexuality. And at the end of the session I said, "How about if we join hands and say a little prayer?" She said, "I don't believe in God." Her eyes were "checking me out" for a reaction. She then asked, "How do you feel about what I just told you, that I don't believe in God? You, a priest, just spent an hour with me. You just shot an hour with me! How do you feel about that?" I said, "I'm not really upset about that right now. I now know a little bit about your life and what you're dealiing with, and I understand that you don't believe in God.

But I'd be very upset if I thought God did not believe in you." That's part one. Do all you can to lead the woman to see that God believes in her. "God still loves you; God wants to heal you." Part two then comes when the woman can say, "I believe in God." We can't give what we don't have. The woman who experiences God's grace-filled gift of love is then empowered to believe in Him Who has given the gift of Himself.

For some this is called the "born-again" experience, for others "being saved," for others, "walking with the Lord" or living in the state of grace. Whatever be the name or nuance, the reality is basically the same: a personal experience of and relationship with Jesus Christ.

If we are Christians and members of the Body of Christ, it is much to your friend's benefit to know that we do not represent only ourselves in the healing process for many others are praying with us for her. Her healing and reconciliation will not just be with her God, the Father, and Jesus, the Son, and the Holy Spirit. It will also be with His Body, the community of the church, in whom we are all brothers and sisters.

If we are Catholic Christians, we have a particularly powerful tool for healing in the Sacrament of Reconciliation. In truth, we don't need others to heal and forgive. God can do it anytime and anywhere He wants. Our faith history tells us, however, that God saves in community — be it the people of Israel or the New Israel, the church. He uses the community of the church and His representatives to proclaim him as a healing God. If the sacrament of Reconciliation can be integrated into the healing process at an appropriate time, the woman will hopefully realize that healing does not just consist of her reaching up and out, but God the Father, in Jesus, reaching down, as we said before.

In particular, the role of the priest in the Sacrament is to definitively proclaim God's healing to a sister in Christ. The priest is no better than she, for he, too, is a sinner. In fact, it is God's irony and choice that he uses the broken to announce his wholeness, the fellow sinner to announce the presence of He who was without sin. The healing power of the priest is not his own. Of himself he has no power. His authority comes from the community of the church. Thus he represents not himself only, but

Jesus, the founder of the community whose healing word he bears. His authority to proclaim that healing is the Carpenter of Nazareth, the Christ whose presence the community is to embody.

The sacrament of Reconciliation provides a unique time in a person's faith history when Christ is encountered through the mediation of the church community and the priest as the ordained representative of that community. The priest, a fellow pilgrim on this journey of healing, is gifted with the privilege of welcoming the woman back to full union with the church community. He is much more so a healer than a judge. He is a proclaimer of the Lord's mercy.

If the woman can be led to see the sacrament in this way, a healing *with* her God *through* His community, many wounds may be healed. When a human life is lost, the whole human community is the poorer for it. Many a woman has wondered during her time of torment if her child might not have grown up to find the cure for cancer or make a great contribution to world peace. Idle fantasy and speculation? To us, perhaps. But to the woman who grieves and shares her regrets it tells us in yet another way of the depth of her pain in blocking a destiny and destroying a dream. There are many priests, ministers, rabbis, and clergypersons that are very sensitive to the plight of the woman who has had an abortion. Religious bodies should do more to help identify them and when necessary, provide specialized training.

3. Seeing the Story

Helping your friend to look back over the whole situation is important. Greater clarity and understanding may come with the passing of time. "*How* did it happen? *Why* did it happen? *What* have I learned from it? *What* are the kinds of personalities, both male and female, that I'm vulnerable to, that I listen to, that I trust? Is it the soft voice, blond hair, blue eyes, or build that sets me up every time?" Help your friend learn by her mistakes, that she might not repeat them. Challenge her: "What can I do to prevent a recurrence of this pain?" And when this pain is reasonably healed, do I really understand that God wishes to use His community to heal me? God uses flesh to heal flesh. God uses blood to heal blood. God uses life to heal life. If the woman begins to understand that foundation of faith, that God uses Christ Incarnate among us to heal each other, then as a Catholic, we've begun to understand the theological basis for sacramentality. Some Catholics struggle with the concept of a mere man, a priest, in the Sacrament of Reconciliation or Confession. The deeper question is to understand a God who can use a broken, weak, sometimes corrupt community, as it journeys through human history, for His saving purposes. I think of this whole process as a living "Eucharistia," a living Thanksgiving. Whenever God heals, the story of the Prodigal Son and the Loving Father (Luke 15) is retold and relived. When the Gospels speak of Eucharist, we are reminded that we, too, are bread. Jesus *chose* bread, *blessed* it, *broke* it, and *gave* it. This woman was *chosen* a long time ago to be conception, creation, life. At her Baptism she was *blessed,* set aside as special and invited to share in the mystery of Life itself, death, and resurrection. And then, through the abortion, she was *broken.* Truly, the seeds of her life have been scattered on many hillsides. But now, through this healing, through the instrumentality of you and me, a part of God's community, she's called to be *given.*

What we do at the Lord's Table is to be a reflection of what we do in each other's lives. Our worship is not something external to reality or extraneous to it. It's at the very core of it. We have a relational God. If we understand His process of giving life to us in human history and through His Church Communities, then we'll understand ourselves as broken but true vehicles of His call to rebuild and renew his family.

4. Grieving

As a woman begins to grieve over her lost child, she now more closely comes in contact with the reality of what she has done, the actual consequences of her actions. Her darkest hour may come right before the dawn. *Her* child has been lost. The justification for the abortion may have been rooted in a depersonification of the child. The healing cannot be. She may now need to see the child as a person and even name the child. She may need to imagine what the child looked like, describe the child, and even pray for or to the child. Most importantly, she may need to ask the child's forgiveness for having aborted not just a child but "my son" or "my daughter."

Let the tears flow freely here if need be. Perhaps not only hers, but yours as well for most certainly you have now entered into the inner sanctum of a friend's deepest pain and loss. Since you care, since this child was made in the image and likeness of our Loving God, you, too, mourn the loss with this mother.

When you sense the moment is right, ask her to close her eyes and visualize her child, laughing or smiling on God our Father's, or Jesus' lap, hugged and held safe and warm. Ask her to speak to her child, and ask forgiveness from the child. "You were filled with a sorrow that came from God, sorrow for God's sake produces a repentance without regrets, leading to salvation, whereas worldly sorrow brings death." (2 Cor. 7:9-10) This sorrow, then, and grieving over her loss can be a very freeing and healing experience. It is *not* merely a psychological technique, for it is experienced in the context of prayer and dialogue with Jesus, the Father and the Spirit. The woman is speaking from her heart, but that is only part of it. For in faith we believe *the Lord* listens and receives her pain unto Himself. Here it might be very appropriate to read one of the Scripture passages relating Jesus' special and tender love for children. " . . . he embraced them and blessed them, placing his hands on them." (Mark 10:16) The beauty and spiritual irony in this may well be that a mother (and I use that word intentionally, for a woman is a mother long before she gives birth to her child) who has aborted her child may be led to healing precisely through an understanding of who that child is to God and to herself. "Let the children come to me and do not hinder them. It is to such as these that the Kingdom of God belongs." (Mark 10:14) Her child has come to the Lord. God has given the child an eternal spark that even the abortionist cannot destroy. That very child will lead her to Him as well.

Though it is not very common, it does sometimes happen that a child is conceived in a rape situation. The woman who seeks healing, and grieves the loss of her child's life, has come to a degree of insight from that violent pain. For now she knows that the manner of a child's conception does not alter the sacredness of his life. In other words, a child's life is no less sacred because of the manner of his conception. A child born of a violent rape is just as sacred to God as a child born of a happy marriage, entitled to be loved and wanted. And a woman who presently seeks healing now knows well that he has not found a problem pregnancy "solved" nor her own inner peace at the price of her child's life.

If she is a young teenager she may also reflect on the many who told her to "act like a woman, deciding for yourself, do what *you* want to do," without leading her to counsellors and other informative resources that would have helped her understand the very possible and common biological, physical, and psychological consequences of her decision, as well as the spiritual "fall-out" and ongoing pain and suffering. Perhaps they, too, didn't know better, or perhaps they didn't have the courage to tell her something that, at the time, she didn't want to hear. Few of those who encourage the abortion tend to remain and support the girl in the aftermath of its consequences. Another lesson of life learned.

5. Healed and Whole

What can we say of the actual healing experience itself? What is it like? What

Healing happens not only when the person reaches up and out but when he or she grasps God's hand as he reaches down. Then grace and nature are once again joined.

signs accompany the healing from an abortion? How do we define a whole and restored life? What differences and growth will the woman sense and feel within herself? Let us try to shed a little light on these questions.

Even though a woman may intellectually understand God's love for her and her right in His eyes to be healed because of that love, that is not the essence nor the totality of the healing. Healing brings integration and restoration. It is a time when the head and the heart come together. What is believed in the mind is felt and grasped in the heart. It is a time when the woman is finally able to give herself permission to feel good again. Up until that point, she often feels an impulsive need to keep punishing herself. "It is not right that I feel good again. I must continue to suffer for the horrible thing that I have done." The time of healing brings a sense of inner peace and a profound yet gentle feeling of being forgiven. The past is not forgotten but it is overshadowed and put in perspective by the deeper reality of the Father's love. It is a time when the woman allows God to be God and His will to replace her own. Divine love replaces self condemnation. She believes and feels that her "cry to be whole" has been heard by him. God's words have taken root seriously in her heart and the message is not unlike that of Isaiah 40:1. "Speak to the heart of Jerusalem and call to her that her time of service is ended, that her sin is atoned for. . ." The broken woman is no longer broken. She is no longer a slave and in bondage to her impulsive need for self-punishment. The woman now realizes that she has no right to condemn herself if God has forgiven her.

Healing brings an attitudinal change along with a spiritual change. The "yes, but. . . ." syndrome comes to an end. This is the automatic negative syndrome that continues to pull the woman down. Each time the woman is tempted to forgive herself a voice from deep within cries out and says, "Yes, but always remember what you've done. You cannot be forgiven!" In healing, a deeper voice from within reminds her that she is still the temple of the Spirit, yet beloved by her God. In fact, the voice is ". . . the spirit making intercession for us with groanings that cannot be expressed in speech." (Rom. 8:26)

98

Finally, the other physical and emotional disorders that had their roots in the abortion trauma gradually cease. Healthy sleep patterns and dietary habits are restored. Emotional stability and a sense of self-worth and self-esteem returns. Healing takes place when tears come not so much because the past is painfully remembered, but because the present now carries with it the Father's hope and love. Paul's words of Romans 8:28 are understood in a new way as never before: ". . . all things work together for those who love God. . . ." Even this, Lord? Yes, my child, even this.

Reflections

1. "God helps those who stop hurting themselves." What does this statement mean to you?

2. What prevents a woman from believing that God really *wants* to heal her?

3. Do you feel a woman must have the experience of God believing in and loving her to be healed?

4. "God uses life to heal life." How do you want God to use you in the abortion healing process?

5. Viewing yourself as a living "Eucharistia," where are you at this point in your life: chosen, blessed, broken, or given?

6. Do others' tears and intense pain make you feel uncomfortable? How do you handle them?

7. "A child's life is no less sacred because of the manner of his conception." What does this statement say to you?

8. Recall a time in your life when you felt healed. Describe the feeling and the meaning of it.

5. The Future of the Healing Process

What will the future bring? An ongoing support system and positive relationships are extremely important as a follow-up. WEBA (Women Exploited by Abortion) is an excellent example of this. The groups can be an excellent vehicle for a woman, within a confidential setting, to share her story with those who have been there. The sharing of faith is an important part of the story, but mutual respect for one another's faith must be maintained. A woman of another faith, for example, in the midst of a session, may ask, "Why are you doing this? What's behind it? What do you want?" I'll gladly share my Catholic faith with her and my relationship with Christ. My hope is that she'll be a better Baptist, Methodist, Episcopalian, etc., because I've *shared* my identity with her, not because I've tried to manipulate her out of her own. I find this type of hidden agenda intellectually and spiritually dishonest. If, without coercion or pressure, a woman indicates an interest to know more about the Catholic faith and wishes to pursue that interest, I am delighted to respond. But my commitment to her healing process is not contingent upon her interest in my Church. "I'll get her healed, and then I'll score one for Jesus because next Sunday she's going to be in that first pew at MY church." I've seen this happen. It's sad. The woman's already been exploited enough! The Lord doesn't manipulate, and He doesn't need us to do it for Him. He invites and so should we.

During a recent retreat I was conducting for families, a woman stood up, and with tears in her eyes, shared her relationship with Jesus Christ and how she came to it. She said, "I was born and raised a Catholic, went through nine years of Catholic school, but never really had a personal experience of Jesus Christ. Then I went on a Discovery weekend, and I experienced Jesus Christ on that retreat. I left that retreat and started going to a Baptist church with my boyfriend, who was Baptist, now my husband. And my husband and baby and I are Baptists and we love it, and I want to thank Father Mike!" The Lord works in strange ways!

Professional Counselling

If necessary we can use the trust bond
we've established with our friend as a lever
to lead her to professional counselling. If
we've been effective in activating this
process, but there's more healing needed,
refer the woman to a professional
counsellor as a follow-up. Compose a list of
professionals that you trust and know
integrate Christian values into their
counselling. The "If it feels good, do it!"
philosophy is not adequate. If it was, the
woman would not have had the abortion in
the first place. If we've been in the pro-life
movement long enough we've come to hear
the common accusation, "You're just trying
to impose your morality on me." We're not
trying to impose. We're trying to proclaim
and protect the sacredness of His children's
lives. Through a sharing of faith, we're
facilitating a healing process.

Strength Of Conviction

If the woman wants to reject our words,
she certainly can. But we can still have the
strength of our own convictions. We can
say to the woman, "I believe in life. This is
the way I choose to love you, and try to heal

you." To the woman who's contemplating an abortion, "I know you didn't come to me, thinking that I was going to say, 'If you want to have an abortion, it's okay.' You know that I believe that if you have that abortion the pain that will result will be immeasurably more severe than any pain you'd go though if you carried the child to term." We can state that. The woman appreciates that honesty. I once heard of an interesting experience of a pro-life speaker in a public high school. The majority of the students were pro-abortion at first but then reconsidered. A girl came up to the speaker and said, "You know, we have all sorts of guest speakers who come in and check us out to see what we want to hear, and then they tell us what they think we want to hear. You've changed some minds here today because you stuck to your guns and told us what you really believe and why." Youth today do respect us for sticking up for our convictions and remaining true to them. We can do that and still respect them and us.

Dependency

Be conscious and cautious of the possibility of an unhealthy dependency which may stifle, rather than enhance the woman's growth. We must not let our need to be needed take precedence over the woman's need to grow and be free. Healing is freedom. Otherwise, all we will do is lead her to trade one type of dependency and brokenness for another. And we will be that other dependency. Be aware of what is happening between you.

A Guide

This healing process is something that I find has worked very well for me over the last several years. Please do not view it as a rigid and juridical formula to follow. It is not. It is a guideline, one way of many to guide a woman through a healing process. The most precious resource or gift God has given the broken woman is you: your personality, your compassion, your sensitivity, your honesty, your openness, your love, your God. That's Number 1. The other things I've shared with you are things that build upon *who* you are. Use my words as a help but your gifts and love as the basis. Pray, reflect, respond. Ask a couple of close friends, who have worked with you and who know your gifts, to share

The author of life is one who
must heal the loss of life

with you the strengths and weaknesses they see in you. Take those suggestions to heart.

A Commitment To Life

When is a woman ready to make a commitment to the pro-life cause, if ever? What are the signs? Even when a woman who has had an abortion comes forward willingly and volunteers to speak or give witness to her personal tragedy, how can we decide if she is ready?

First, true healing should bring a pro-life vision that expands from concern for the pre-born stage of life to all other life stages and situations. Thus, a woman healed of an abortion may not necessarily fulfill her need to serve the cause of life by specifically working with the abortion issue. Poverty, hunger, unemployment, the environment, the nuclear question are just a few of the many social-justice and life issues at root. Any and all of these are valid expressions of proclaiming the sacredness of life, and ultimately enhance the need to see the sacredness of the unborn.

A woman is ready to make a commitment

to the pro-life cause when she comes forward not out of guilt but from free-willed and healed conviction. She does not have to "make up" for anything. She seeks to serve that she might help prevent her sisters from making the same mistake she has made.

Pro-life people in leadership positions must be willing to put the woman's emotional needs and spiritual maturity as a unique person before their own organizational needs or plans. As I alluded to earlier, in Chapter 1, to not do so is to exploit her again — this time by the very forces committed to healing her! She may have a *need* for greater involvement but privacy as well. She has the *right* not to be exploited. We must consider her family's feelings, how her friends will react, her other priorities, (e.g. husband, children, job, etc.) and how her involvement will most likely affect her. Will the people who mean the most to her be behind her? If a sufficient period of time between the healing process and the involvement has not passed, a fragile stability and tenuous spiritual growth might set her back considerably. This is especially true if her involvement has to do with publicly sharing her story. Even more practically, will she be reasonably compensated, financially or otherwise, for the time and personal expense that her participation might involve? It is not fair that she suffer a hardship as she dedicates herself to help others.

All these questions and their answers are crucial considerations for any decison about a woman's pro-life involvement. If they are faced honestly, openly, and prayerfully *by* all concerned the result would be truly pro-life *for* all concerned.

A Prayer For Healing

God, our Father, we thank you for the gift of life. You chose to bless us with the gift that has been given freely, and now we are called to give it freely. Give us a sense of compassion, love, and healing. Give us a sense of openness and understanding that we might be Your instruments. Father, we make so many mistakes. We're human, and sometimes we fail. Sometimes we want to walk in front of everyone, and at times we're scared and fearful and want to pause and walk far behind. It's at those times that You remind us that You wish to send Your Son to walk beside us and be our friend. "Do not let your hearts be troubled, trust in God, trust in Me. In My Father's house there are many rooms." Father, for the woman today who needs healing, we pray that by the grace of our words and Your love that healing might take place. For the children that have come to you through the pain of abortion, welcome them home, Father, with mercy, love, compassion, and tenderness. Rejoice in Your house, for they are Your special angels, Your sons and daughters. Together one day we will be with them. Let their innocence, Lord, remind us of Your call in our hearts to be pure, holy, and innocent.

"If I knew then what I know now, you would never have died, my child. I'd have held you close and nurtured you, and kept you by my side. I'd have sung you songs and treasured you more than silver, more than gold. But this song is all I'll ever give to the babe I'll never hold. I've never written poetry that hasn't been a praise to the Lord Who wept with me and held me through those days. Jesus, now I'm asking, I know you hear my plea. Please hold my babe for me." (Special thanks to WEBA for the use of this prayer.)

Father, we give You thanks, God of Life. Call us to celebrate that life, now and forever. Amen.

". . . this is what God asks of you: only this, to act justly, to love tenderly and to walk humbly with your God." (Micah 6:8)

Reflections

1. "We must not let our need to be needed take precedence over the woman's need to grow and be free." How do you feel about this statement in terms of your own needs and wants?

2. What would be *your* prayer for a woman who has been healed of an abortion with your help?

The contents of this book are also available in videocassette and audiotape.

For information, please contact 1-800-821-7926.